Whiskey Island: Literary Biographies

Virginia Aronson

ISBN: 978-93-6354-490-1

First Edition: 2025
Rs. 200/-

Cyberwit.net
HIG 45 Kaushambi Kunj, Kalindipuram
Allahabad - 211011 (U.P.) India
http://www.cyberwit.net
E-mail: info@cyberwit.net

Printed at Repro.

Contents

James Baldwin	5
John Cheever	12
F. Scott Fitzgerald	20
Ian Fleming	29
Dashiell Hammett	38
Ernest Hemingway	48
James Joyce	52
Norman Mailer	58
Biographies	64
References	74
Recommended Reading	75
Acknowledgments	76

Whisky, I find, helps clarity of thought. And reduces pain.
It has the additional virtue of making you drunk or,
if taken in sufficient quantity, very drunk.
—Julian Barnes, *The Sense of an Ending*

James Baldwin
(1924-1987)

The Poor are Always Crossing the Sahara

Feeling invisible in America
James Arthur Jones Baldwin
Jimmy to his friends, step-
father a preacher, angry
fiery man who stood
Jimmy in the pulpit
at 14
at 17
writer, dropout, menial
factory jobs, meatpacking
elevator boy and janitor
earning money to help
support seven siblings
on the streets of Harlem
that storm inside
...the roar rising
from the void.

A lifelong workaholic
voice full of elegance
in essays, novels
short stories and plays on
masculinity and sexuality
race, class, human rights
civil rights, gay rights
the cultural obstacles
to social acceptance
...whatever's in me
I didn't put there. And
I can't take it out.

As a member of a minority
within a minority

within a minority
artist
queer
black
in a country condemning
all that he was
he left
for France
for freedom

to be visible
to be himself.

Go Tell It on the Mountain

Chilling in the pulpit
unspeakably cruel at home
his step-father engendered
a murderous bitterness
anger building force
to take out with him
to the white world
where he had nothing
and no identity
I was born dead.

Outside Harlem
the bias of Southerners
the rules of Jim Crow
the rage burned inside
the hatred he carried
in his heart he moved
to Greenwich Village
artists and bohemians
white and black
gay and straight
writing, writing
trying to work it all out.

On the day her husband died
Jimmy's mother gave birth
to their eighth child
on the day of the funeral
Jimmy drank whiskey
at the empty church
life and death
so close together
like love and hate

his step-father's legacy:
nothing is escaped.

People are trapped
in history
and history is trapped
in them.

Trouble Means You're Alone

I want to be an honest man
and a good writer.

He arrived in France
with forty dollars
no savings
no French
nights in sordid hotels
days in expat cafés
writing tragic stories
his characters stuck
in the cage of reality:
They got us in a trick
bag, baby.

Life-changing obsession
with a white teenage boy
who married a black actress
leaving him flailing
a self-destroying limbo
suicide or harsh reality:
facing who he was
a small, slight man
charming, entertaining
big eyes, big grin
his stature growing
on the cover of *Time*
the voice of black America
literary, wild and cool

or drunk, depressed
writing, always writing
with morality, humanity

clarity, brevity, *baby*
we are gonna burn it down.

A big house on a hill
in the south of France
Johnny Walker Black
all night long
typing, typing
to change the world
an honest man
a good writer
still relevant today.

John Cheever
(1912-1982)

The Cheever Chronicle

This is a story to be read in bed
in an old house on a rainy night.

Father a successful businessman
who loved Shakespeare, storytelling
but made terrible investments
lost their home, sobriety
his mother ran a gift shop
in their small Boston 'burb
John dropped out of school
lonely, awkward outsider
drowning his shy despair
in four fingers of gin
and a jovial impersonation
of the man he wished to be:
a writer with a pretty wife
from a well-to-do family
leading a charmed life.

Oh ho.

The Chekhov of the Suburbs
dean of contemporary American
stories like miniature novels
about the Upper East Side
Westchester suburbs
old New England villages
where residents upheld decorum
while hiding their corruption
and much marital misery
he took on the mantle
of the country squire

poverty and insecurity
stalking him all his life.

The Cheevers in Manhattan

In the tall apartment building
all the well-heeled husbands
in the morning elevator
on the way to the office
in Brooks Brothers suits
button-downs, polished shoes
gray felt hats, dapper
riding down to the lobby
they hurried off to jobs
John to the basement
windowless storage room
stripped to his boxers
at a folding table
writing stories
for *The New Yorker.*

Married with a daughter
he published his stories
tried to make a living
and escape his heritage
his father dead from booze
grandfather too
brother a bad drunk
the Cheever family curse.

He soaked himself in drink
yearning to be illustrious
yearning for something else
passing through life
in a browned-out fog
while *every comely man,*
every bank clerk and delivery boy

was aimed at my life
like a loaded pistol.

The Cheevers in Westchester

A rental cottage
on a vast green estate
of a country mansion
90 rooms and a ballroom
Tiffany glass, marble floors
old masters on paneled walls.

Surrounded by friends
educated, affluent
heroic drinkers all
morning martinis and laughter
swimming pools and cigarettes
multiple children, lovely wives
who stayed home
in their close community
of honeysuckle, dogwoods
frolicking dogs
chirping tree frogs
elms, willows, rolling
lawns of grazing sheep
a pond for skating in winter.

At the family dinner table
Mother served meals
with a side of bitterness
the siblings squabbling
the family's intense
discussions on books
films, friends, problems
advising and arguing
the occasional explosion
someone storming off…

dinner guests shocked
at their meanness
their ability to forgive
the depth of their devotion
to one another.

The Cheever Scandal

When Mary met John
in an elevator
on Fifth Avenue
on his way to her office
to see his literary agent
she saw a little man
in an oversized jacket
a big warm smile
sparkling blue eyes
she had no idea how
he saw his own life:
either untenable
or transcendent.

His first 50 years
a struggle for stability
professional success
a family, home, children…
and once he had it all
plus fame and fortune
he spent 20 years
trying to free himself
by cheating, getting drunk.

Their bond would loosen
break and mend again
over 40 turbulent years
her affairs, his bisexuality…
still, he needed her love
and she needed his need
as he floundered
for fleeting moments
of transcendence.

F. Scott Fitzgerald
(1896-1940)

The Curious Case of Francis Scott Key Fitzgerald

Celebrated in his 20s
forgotten in his 30s
dead by 44 he lived
his life backward
like the character
in his popular story

one of 164 published
stories and novels written
with style, wit, imagination
on themes of love, success
and failure to achieve
the illusive American Dream.

A Midwesterner
half black Irish and
half old American stock
his mother nervous, odd
his father drinking, jobs
businesses gone bust
Scott a poor student
in private schools
among the elite
always the outsider
looking in, wanting in
and resenting the rich
and developing
a two-cylinder
inferiority complex…

Mr. Nobody from Nowhere
charming, endearing
a good friend to many

a victim to his insecurity
alcoholism, depression, debt
self-destructive he flamed out
twenty years before he died.

Gatsbyesque

A Princeton sophomore
Scott fell in love
with a wealthy socialite
and learned the hard way
rich girls don't marry poor boys
a lesson he shared
in his heartbreaking stories
in his heartbroken life.

He wrote his first novel
in the army in Kansas
stationed in Alabama
the officers popular
at dances at country clubs
where he met Zelda Sayre:
red-gold hair, reckless laugh
socially prominent wild child
with all the self-confidence
Fitzgerald lacked.

The war over he lived
in dire squalor
revising his novel
rejected by publishers
over and over
she refused to marry
unless prospects improved
with a publishing contract

they wed in Manhattan
his book a bestseller
the dashing young couple
money, fame, paparazzi

recording their antics:
sliding down banisters
diving in fountains
partying and drinking
Champagne by the magnum

the roaring '20s
the speakeasy era
when life was literally
a dream…racing along
under its own power, served
by great filling stations
full of money.

Beautiful and Damned

They moved to Long Island
the lush background
for *The Great Gatsby*
novel he wrote
in expat Paris
St. Raphaël, the Riviera
completed in Rome.

Despite critical acclaim
sales remained poor
their finances dwindling
he was easily lured
by Hollywood dazzle
big cash for scripts.

Crazy about the baby
their daughter Scottie
the happy couple
'til Zelda lost her mind
threw herself down stairs
torched her ball gowns
in the hotel bathtub.

So he moved them away
to a big old mansion
on the Delaware River
to bring a judicious tranquility
to stop fighting, drinking
and focus on his craft.

But Zelda tried to drive
off a cliff in France
set fire to their home

a purveyor of chaos
hospitalized repeatedly
in and out and in
clinics, institutions

Scott waiting nearby
drinking, worrying
writing to pay the bills
for his wife and child:
in a real dark night of the soul
it is always three o-clock in the morning,

The Far Side of Paradise

For additional income
for Zelda in the wards
Scottie in boarding school
Scott went west
to the Hollywood studios

drinking with Bogart
Dorothy Parker *et al*
on benders, bedridden
he found a new love
a young gossip columnist
who cared for him
when he couldn't.

His books out of print
sleeping pills worn off
the uppers kicking in
strong coffee by the pot
he began a new novel
about a movie mogul
about one man's end…

but a fatal heart attack
his own life unfinished.

An old Princeton friend
completed the manuscript
for *The Last Tycoon*
bound in one volume
with the forgotten Gatsby
a paperback double feature
sent to American soldiers
fighting in World War II.

And *The Great Gatsby*
a massive success
an all-American classic
still selling to this day.

Once a forgotten writer
struggling to support family
obscurity his fate…
achieving immortality
his dream coming true
after he was gone.

The poor son of a bitch.

Ian Fleming
(1908-1964)

Ian the Black Sheep

The second of four Fleming
brothers with a hero father
an *über*-wealthy grandfather
an overbearing mother.

Oh, Ian the black sheep
moody, withdrawn, long
hair slicked back exuding
the promise of something
dashing or daring, risks
in his piercing blue eyes
great laugh all the girls
flocked to him, his friends
lost out to him at Eton
his future spy network
fatherless boys whose dads
had died in World War I.

He learned German, French
a bit of Russian he decided
he wanted to write novels
but held off, his older brother
a young author and Ian
flunked the diplomat exam
became a writer for Reuters.

Charming, persuasive, magnetic
an iconoclast people liked him
in Moscow to cover a sham
trial of two English businessmen
when he saw the dark hand
of Russia murderous, devious
in his future spy novels and

his book collection growing
he collected women too:
hunt, acquire, shelve.

Oh, the seductive playboy
a smooth rock against which
so many reckless women
dashed themselves.

Ian the Spy

Left out of his grandfather's estate
the only heir without funds
he worked for a living
for newspapers, banks
and a job as a personal aid
to the director of Naval Intelligence
laying the groundwork
for the greatest intel alliance
in history he helped build
the CIA as well
but never talked
about what he did he did
start to drink too much
during the war.

His 450 operatives
captured Enigma machines
to decode Nazi plans
the life or death drama, the risks
he recreated while managing
a newspaper syndicate
during the Cold War
a global cadre
of reporter spies
saving the world
from Russian aggression.

He rose to the challenge
for the rush, oh the rush
that incandescent high
one only experiences
in a moment of greatness
he was able to recapture

with his writing
in his novels
on the risks, the wins
against the evil empire
by the glamorous Brit
the dapper super-spy

double-oh seven
James Bond.

Ian at Goldeneye

He fell in love with
the rum punch on arrival
the fresh fruits, fresh fish
the colors, scents, trees
swaying palms and mangos
warm rain on warm waves
caressing the white sand
on the island of Jamaica.

He'd lost his first love
a sweet Swiss girl
at his mother's demand
then Muriel, his love
a motorcycle dispatcher
killed in the war
his married older lover
Maud warned him
no, not Ann.

Lady Ann, chaos Ann
he liked her independence
her toughness he said
she was such a bitch.

On fourteen acres north
of Montego Bay
he built his home
with money from Maud
no glass in the windows
big sky, turquoise sea
blue floors and birds
flying in and out
he called it Goldeneye.

Ann visiting, leaving
a son her husband
believed was his own
divorce and a marriage
Ian didn't want, violent
whippings he maybe did.

Ian as James Bond

Swimming in clear water
above parrot fish, barracuda
escaping into a hidden world
under deadline he sits down
at his battered Royal typewriter
with *the mind of a sexy boy scout*
introducing a British ultra-hero
attractive to men and women
dangerous, exciting, patriotic
the ultimate suave spy:
himself but romanticized
a fast car fantasy life:
sharp clothes, fine foods
whiskey, gin, martinis
a string of bedworthy girls
a chain of cigarettes
in solitude, darkness
Scottish melancholy.

After the first sale
a Bond every year
all done the same way:
an early morning swim
then hours in the study
two months in Jamaica
editing in Manhattan
retyping in England
one after another until
even JFK would ask:
"What would Bond do?"

Finishing the first book
the bang-bang, kiss-kiss

he hands in the manuscript
in time to marry Ann
and suffers for twelve years
writing eleven more books
smoking, drinking, escaping
her mockery, his depression
before the final chapter
of his film-worthy life:

a glass of whiskey and
dead at the height of fame.

Dashiell Hammett
(1894-1961)

Sam

Samuel Dashiell Hammett
born on a tobacco farm
his mother a De Shiell
with a tubercular cough
father a hard drinker
womanizer, failure
Sam a dropout at 14
to help pay the bills
messenger, paperboy
dockworker, junior clerk
in an advertising office.

At 21 an operative
detective, gumshoe, sleuth
in dirty streets, gritty dens
of thieves, pimps, bootleggers
the Pinkerton Detective Agency
their unblinking eye the motto
"We Never Sleep"
giving rise to the term
private eye.

He had to be cool, discrete
collecting details firsthand
shadowing, garbage picking
pulling break-ins, snooping
and writing up reports:
clear, understated
matter-of-fact memos
descriptions of rogues
lowlifes, liars and scammers
their tricks and tales, stories
he later used to create

his own brand of fiction
with a tough, cinematic style.

He moved murder stories
out of stuffy drawing rooms
into the back alleys
where crime really lives
inventing a new fiction:
the literary detective story
giving birth to film noir.

Dash

The whippet-thin redhead
rolled his own cigarettes
at his black Underwood
typing up stories, smoking
and coughing up blood
the result of a stint
in the Army Ambulance Corps
the Spanish flu, TB

weakened, too ill
for the mean streets
of Pinkertons' Frisco
a port town of wine flats
speakeasies and whores
fog in the hills, ferry horns
mournful and haunting.

He took classes in typing
studied detective magazines
discovered an audience
for his authentic voice
for his deadpan dialogue
his gamey street parlance
the stark charm of an ultra-
masculine sleuth, hiding
a romantic heart—
the urban hero myth
and a brand new genre:
authentic hard-boiled crime.

A success, fame, he lived
between coasts and lives:
Manhattan with lovers

L.A. with his family
his wife and two girls.

His daughters got postcards
clothes, gifts, short visits
dinner with movie stars
bedtime stories and feeling
the dent in Daddy's head
where he got hit with a brick
after bungling a tail job
and the bulge in his hand
the knife tip still there
embedded in his palm.

Ernest Hemingway
(1899-1961)

The Sun Rises

He lived in a world of spirits:
animal spirits
place spirits
writing spirits
the spirits of wine and gin
whiskey and his own high
spirits or the Black Ass
depression that killed him
finally the spirits
did him in.

His seven famous novels
and beloved short stories
on love and war
wilderness adventure
death and freedom
in a world without hope
virile men like himself
in lean, athletic prose
tight dialogue, action
cinematic snapshot scenes
rhythmic from a childhood
of cello, orchestra and
the terse sentences
of journalism jobs.

If he wrote it
he could get rid of it.
He had gotten rid
of many things
by writing them.

Hunting, fishing, camping
enthralled with nature
wounded in two wars
and by his first love
he would leave first
before his wives
before his mind
left him alone
with the spirits.

A Moveable Feast

Hadley had a breakdown
and hid at home
her father a suicide
after her mother died
she met Ernest, Hem
kind of knocked people over
his potential right out
in the open she told him
The world's a jail, and
we're going to break it
together with her money
in a trust he liked her
red-gold hair in Paris
low rent, cheap food, cafés
where there was a way of living
well and working, no matter
how poor you were...

A beautiful romantic city
for a foreign correspondent
training ground with Gertrude
Stein, Pound, Picasso, wine
drinking with James Joyce
traveling with Fitzgerald
to bullfights, fist fights
he wrote it all down
war time vignettes
his first novel a hit
he became the voice
of the Lost Generation
father of son Jack
unpublished work lost
with Hadley's luggage.

Decades later, the father
of three sons, on his fourth
wife told to repossess
two old steamer trunks
stored at the Paris Ritz
full of his notebooks
a young man's struggle
to write one true sentence

his life spread out then
before him
a veritable feast.

Key West

Pauline wrote for Paris *Vogue*
and called him Papa
gave him two more sons
a home in Key West
with a carriage house
converted to a studio
where he could be alone
at his stand-up desk
a salt-water pool
a fishing boat
a lot of booze.

Key West had charm
frame houses, dirt alleys
Conch town characters
grits and boiled grunts
azure skies, sparkling
high seas and quiet
everything a man needed
to write except
to be alone

and he felt
the death loneliness
at the end of every day
wasted not writing
at Sloppy Joe's bar
his fans found him
and Martha Gellhorn
hot war correspondent
the red-gold hair he loved
her: *We are two*

great people. We can
shake the world.

Only later he knew
if you lie with one
against another
you'll do it again
and he left Key West
traded away
what remained
of his life.

Kafka's Cuba

Martha discovered it:
rundown, overgrown
fifteen acres near Havana
full of colorful characters
nightlife, fishing
affordable, lush, exotic
mango trees, royal palms
purple jacaranda, orchids
in bloom he fell in love
with Cuba, out of love
with his wife.

Time writer Mary Welsh
heiress, adventurer
his eventual caretaker
she built a tower
for their Cuban home
for their thirty cats
a top floor city view
the office for Papa

now lying, fighting, wild
spending, grandiose
drinking day and night
and Castro's revolution
a Kafka nightmare
of nationalization, his home
lost and poor Papa
in turmoil, in exile
in Ketchum, Idaho.

The Old Man

Deep in the African bush
two plane crashes
in two days, the first hit
a flock of ibis, the second
exploded on the runway

his skull fractured, dislocated
shoulder, crushed discs
ruptured liver and kidney
he lost sight, lost hearing
lucidity, memory
laughing while reading
his own obit
in the national news.

Fragile, frail, aged
too soon he wrote
The Old Man and the Sea
in eight weeks for *Life*
selling five million copies
winning a Pulitzer
the Nobel Prize
while his mania slid
into years of depression.

When his father shot himself
many years before
Papa had said
I'll probably go
the same way.

And he did.

James Joyce
(1882-1941)

Joyce's Dublin

Father a tenor, raconteur
a man about the pubs
losing jobs, blowing income
hence the inevitable slide
from a comfortable home
with maids and a piano
cut glass, white tablecloths
to *slobland*, offal, trash
inkpots by *seaspawn*
cocklepickers subsisting
on tea, bread-'n'-drippin'
the ten Joyce children
living in near slums

while "Sunny Jim"
nearsighted singer, smart
voracious reader at school
the Jesuits and their strictures
appealed before he rebelled
with trips to Nighttown
to visit the whores
to drink to excess
to *exult in sin*
in his frayed clothing
torn shoes, sailor cap
singing for refills
so full of himself
unlike most Irish boys
he believed in his future

in Paris he drank, wrote
in bars, cafés, cheap rooms

serious but unpublished
for another ten years.

Joyce and Nora

After his mother died
back in Dublin drinking
he met Nora Barnacle
jaunty auburn-haired
maid from Galway
country girl, peasant
not interested in books
spoke in riddles, prickly
stories of Catholic girlhood
he found enchanting.

On June the 16th
on their first *walking out*
they strolled by the river
to the green gray bay
behind the granite rocks
she took him in her mouth
and he wanted her more
for the next thirty-five years
from crisis to crisis
illness and madness
poverty, fame and fortune.

Unmarried, scandalous
they ran off together
Zürich, Trieste, Rome
teaching English all day
tavernas, caffés all night
in hotel rooms waiting
Nora and the baby
Nora and two babies
taking in laundry
ironing, burning

mad at her mate
not working enough
always working on writing.

She was his Ireland
limestone and grass
harp and shamrock
his rock, his muse
caretaker, queen
crowned heart
turf and bog
his barnacle goose.

Joyce's Ulysses

He wrote he said
to tell the truth
about Ireland…but
the publishers feared
libel, obscenity laws
so he kept on writing
half blind in dark rooms
on a voyage to the new
he pushed further out
for *Ulysses*, further still
for *Finnegans Wake.*

Some panned his novels
as the scribblings of a madman
while others named him
the greatest writer
of his time
on the cover of *Time*
in a smoking jacket
in London to get married
to Nora before the war
in exile in Zürich
an eye patch, an ulcer
perforated, dead.

Ireland refused his body
as he had rejected them
when he made poetry
his sacrament, his purpose
his truth, his life goal
to reinvent his Dublin
in the poignant details
of everyday life.

Norman Mailer
(1923-2007)

Norman Kingsley Mailer

Jews from Lithuania
his father's family fled
to South Africa
ran successful businesses
but Norman's dad went bad
gambled, embezzled, fled
to the US and married
a hardworking young woman
at her family's hotel
on a New Jersey beach.

With their baby Norman
the Mailers moved
to seedy Brooklyn
to growing debt
to the gangsters
but their prodigy
admitted early
to Harvard
studying literature
in love with lowlife
realism, modernism
smoking and drinking
a conspicuous outsider
reckless, unconventional.

He adopted a persona:
the wildman writer
hardnosed, cool, edgy
army veteran with valor
and the desire to write
about his fellow soldiers

in long letters to Bea
the first of six wives.

In a uniquely erudite
roughneck style
he punched his way
down the rough road
to fame
and infamy.

The Wives of Norman Mailer

You can become a different man
in each marriage.

Beatrice a blind date
foul-mouthed Boston girl
introduced Mailer
to Marxism, politics
he gave her a tin ring
he bought for 25 cents.

First novel a bestseller
they lived in Paris
moved to Hollywood
had a daughter
summered in Provincetown
a farmhouse in Vermont

until he met Adele Morales
promiscuous, polyamorous
partying with the Beats
the stars, the men and
he hit her, beatings
after a bottle of bourbon
daily weed, tranquilizers
Seconal for sleep.

Living in Greenwich Village
making a run for mayor
he stormed into their home
during a fundraiser
stabbing his wife twice
once in the back

once in the chest
close to the heart

she did not press charges
stayed and thought
that's what it costs
to be married
to a genius

until he met
a conservative heiress
a one-year wife

until he met
Beverly Bentley
and had two sons
a big house on the beach
in Provincetown

until she left him
sleeping with a jazz singer
mother of his seventh child
in western Mass, visiting

throughout his marriages
another mistress in LA

throughout all his wives
even the lovely last, Norris
26 like his eldest daughter

she stayed for 30 years
of affairs, drunks, fights
two more sons and
they all lived together

in a New York brownstone
in a house in Ptown
one big happy family
unhappy in the Mailer way.

I like to marry women
whom I can beat
once in a while,
and who fight back.

Biographies

One of the legends of late 20th century American literature, **James Baldwin** was enigmatic and magnetic, sociable and self-absorbed, funny and depressed, and androgynous (he said), not gay.

Growing up in Harlem, the preacher's step-son became a Youth Minister at 14 and left the church at 17. His religion gave him a literary voice, his love of orating provided solid dramatic skill. Living in Greenwich Village, Jimmy hung around artists in their studios and favorite bars, sleeping with girls and boys and trying to sell his early attempts at a novel. He spoke across chasms to whites and straights, but was continually confronted with injustice and bias.

Moving to France to escape prejudice, he lived there in poverty for the next nine years. Determined not to be categorized as "Negro writer," he published a novel about white characters and the taboo subject of homosexual love.

Afraid of ending up alone or mad, he returned to the US in 1957 and became a spokesperson for civil rights. He had a deep rage and his politics invaded his writing, making him a celebrity. Seeking the privacy he required for writing, he again left the US, this time for Turkey, where he lived throughout the 1960s.

After a serious bout of hepatitis, he recovered in St-Paul de Vence, a quiet village on the Côte d'Azur. He started in on the Johnny Walker Black upon arising ("I am what you'd call a drinking man") and had a great capacity for bourbon too. He made friends in the French village and bought a home there, but was lonely in his last years.

He died of stomach cancer at the age of 63.

Novelist **John Cheever's** lifelong homosexual yearning was masked by the straight suburban world in which he lived and wrote. His stories and novels incorporated this kind of duality as a theme, using a social persona that clashed with internal corruption. His fiction was nostalgic and set in Manhattan's Upper East Side, the Westchester suburbs, and old New England villages.

Cheever grew up in Quincy, Massachusetts, where his father was an alcoholic shoe salesman and his mother ran a gift shop. He dropped out of high school to live in Boston and write stories. He got a job at the writer's colony Yaddo, which became for him a second home.

He married a smart, pretty girl from a wealthy family. His work began appearing regularly in *The New Yorker* (where he would eventually publish 121 stories) but he struggled to pay the bills for his growing family.

While living in Manhattan, he dressed each weekday in a suit and hat, rode the elevator to the lobby with all the businessmen, then spent the morning in the basement in his boxers, writing stories about urbane moralists and unhappy country squires.

The family moved to upstate New York, eventually purchasing a home of their own. When he could no longer hide his alcoholism, he quit drinking, wrote a bestseller about gay love, and was awarded a Pulitzer Prize. He had a series of lovers but remained married (and sober) until his death from cancer at age 70.

Jazz Age writer **F. Scott Fitzgerald** was born in Minnesota as Francis Scott Key Fitzgerald. He was named after the famous American songwriter, his father's cousin.

A Southerner and a heavy drinker, Scott's father repeatedly failed at business and in his sales jobs. The family moved around and rented multiple homes; Scott's friends were wealthy with big houses, so he always felt like an onlooker, an outsider trying to get in. A lifetime of financial struggles bred a deep resentment of the upper class.

At Princeton, Scott spent more time writing and acting in plays than studying, so he failed his classes. He enlisted and spent time in officer training, during which he met Southern debutante Zelda Sayre. She refused to marry him until he published his first novel.

Basking in overnight celebrity, Scott and Zelda Fitzgerald became media darlings due to their Roaring Twenties' antics. But life with Zelda was chaotic and soaked in gin, whiskey, Champagne, and social events that interfered with Scott's work. Struggling for the alone time he needed to write, he managed to publish four novels and four short story collections.

Once Zelda's mental instability became serious, however, Fitzgerald knew his marriage was over. He did not divorce her, though, writing continuously to fund her institutionalizations and their daughter's schooling. He worked in Hollywood and spent his final years with gossip columnist Sheilah Graham.

Fitzgerald suffered a fatal heart attack when he was only 44. At the funeral parlor, Dorothy Parker said, "The poor son of a bitch," a line one of the characters mutters at Gatsby's wake.

Fitzgerald was a romantic and a moralist who embedded his stories with his own convictions on the fleeting beauty of love and youth, and the pitfalls of success and wealth. *The Great Gatsby* is widely regarded as an American classic, Fitzgerald the quintessential 20th century American writer.

British spy novelist **Ian Fleming** led a life full of risk. His grandfather was a poor Scot who became one of the richest men in Great Britain. Ian's father was a war hero in World War I. His older brother wrote bestselling books, while young Ian struggled academically, pulled pranks, and was often in trouble.

While studying languages in Austria with a spy and his novelist wife, Ian decided to be a writer. He began with journalism, working for Reuters and reporting from Moscow, among other locales.

As the personal assistant to the director of Naval Intelligence in World War II, Fleming was hip-deep in espionage. He recreated his role during the Cold War by coordinating a group of journalists to provide intel from around the world. Fleming never spoke of his intelligence work, but he has been credited with helping the US create what would become the Central Intelligence Agency.

Ian Fleming was dashing, romantic, and thrived on danger. He lived on the edge, embarking on multiple love affairs, smoking some 70 cigarettes a day, and drinking excessively. He built a rustic house in Jamaica where he could swim naked, snorkel, and bird watch.

Weeks before marrying a difficult and critical aristocrat, Ian created his alter ego and wrote the first James Bond manuscript. His married life made him despondent, and money was always an issue. Jamaica and James Bond were his best escapes.

Every winter in Jamaica for the last 12 years of his life, he wrote a new Bond novel. The books sold slowly, then volcanically after President Kennedy became a public fan. The Bond movies added to Fleming's fame, which he both enjoyed and loathed.

His lifestyle eventually caught up and Fleming suffered a fatal heart attack at 56. But 007 lives on, an enduring mythical hero.

Modernist **Dashiell Hammett** has been called the dean of the school of hardboiled detective fiction. His influence on literature was immediate and profound, his innovative style adopted by a generation of crime writers. He is credited with inventing the kind of literary crime fiction that was the inspiration for film noir.

Samuel Dashiell Hammett grew up in Baltimore. His father was a drinker and a womanizer, a failure in all of his various businesses. Dash dropped out of school at 14 to help his family, working odd jobs until he was old enough to work as a private detective for the Pinkerton National Detective Agency. Over the years, the company popularized rap sheets, rogue's galleries, mug shots, and fingerprints. The country's oldest and largest detective agency, their operatives collected evidence firsthand via shadowing, digging through garbage, breaking into briefcases, trunks, and homes, and paying people for information.

While in the Army, Dash caught the Spanish flu, and later developed the tuberculosis that would reduce his mobility, introduce him to his wife (a nurse in a veterans hospital), and create the opportunity for his writing career.

He settled in San Francisco, a hotbed of speakeasies and organized crime and the setting for most of his stories. His tubercular lungs weakened him, but he was able to sit and write. So he used what he'd learned as an operative to create rogue detectives who chased down and outsmarted a bevy of local lowlifes. His characters and dialogue were authentic, his style spare, tough, cinematic.

Hammett's life was intense and self-destructive, his heavy drinking, womanizing, gambling, and wild spending alternated with rigorous bouts of disciplined, ascetic, hard work. He bounced between his wife and two daughters in California, the Hollywood highlife, and the New York publishing world. He lived in apartments in upscale hotels on both coasts, got involved with playwright (and big drinker) Lillian Hellman, and joined the Communist Party. His politics would earn him a prison sentence and get his work blacklisted during the McCarthy era.

When he died at age 67, all of his work was out of print. As the executor of Hammett's literary estate, Hellman made it her mission to republish his work. She also published three "memoirs" full of romantic (invented) tales about their secret lives as spies during WWII and the Red Scare. She spent the rest of her life bluffing and taking to court those who accused her of lying. But she succeeded in reviving Dashiell Hammett's reputation, securing his place in the history of literary crime writing.

Ernest Hemingway is famous for his understated prose and economy of words, and for his contributions to the art of the short story. He grew up in Oak Park, Illinois, his father a physician, his mother a musician. He spent summers in northern Michigan, where he hunted, fished, camped, and fell in love with outdoor adventures. He took cello lessons as a child, and was in an orchestra in high school. He wrote for a newspaper at 18. All of these experiences influenced his writing style, which was rhythmic, realistic, detailed, and succinct.

While serving as a volunteer ambulance driver on the Italian front during World War I, he received severe shrapnel wounds in both legs. Upon his return to the US, he wrote freelance articles for a Canadian weekly. He married Hadley Richardson, a financially independent orphan. They spent eight years in Paris and had a son.

After Hemingway published collections of short stories and his first novel *The Sun Also Rises*, he was dubbed the voice of "the lost generation."

He left Hadley for a wealthy writer for Paris *Vogue.* Pauline nicknamed him Papa—and it stuck. They settled in the rustic fishing village of Key West, where her uncle bought them a house with a separate building for Hemingway's writing room. They dug a salt-water pool and he built a boat for big-game fishing and traveling to the Caribbean. Two more sons joined the family.

When home in Key West, Papa often hung out at Sloppy Joe's bar, which is where war correspondent Martha Gellhorn found him. By the end of the 1930s, he had moved with her to a home near Havana. During World War II he covered the European front for *Colliers* magazine. Back at home he chased U-boats as part of a government-sanctioned campaign in the Caribbean.

Hemingway left Martha for his fourth wife, Mary, who became his caretaker as old injuries and heavy drinking began to take a toll. He'd suffered multiple concussions over the years, which eventually changed his behavior. He began to tell wild lies, his moods were erratic, and he was fighting and drinking virtually without cease. His writing deteriorated and he lost lucidity.

Yet Hemingway took only eight weeks to write the classic *The Old Man and the Sea,* based on a story told to him by his boat's first mate. He also managed to write *A Moveable Feast* from old notebooks he'd kept in Paris in the '20s, which was published after his death.

When Castro made living in Cuba problematic, the Hemingways moved to Idaho. Unable to manage his mental health, Hemingway was hospitalized for depression. When he came home from the hospital, he retrieved a shotgun and committed suicide.

The Irish genius **James Joyce** was at one point the most famous writer in the world, but he struggled with poverty for most of his career. He lived off the financial aid of his patrons, the benefactors who believed in the importance of his unique modernist style.

Joyce left Dublin for the continent when he was in his early 20s. He was accompanied by his lifelong companion Nora Barnacle. The couple had two children while bouncing from rundown hotel to hotel. He taught English during the day; at night he would spend his meager earnings in the local cafés and bars. In bleak rooms in Rome, Trieste, Paris, and Zürich, he wrote on a desk made from a suitcase held in his lap.

Joyce had multiple operations on his eyes until he was almost blind. He wore an eye patch, and did his writing in the dark using colored pens. While living in Switzerland, Joyce died from a perforated ulcer. He was 58.

Even though his world-famous work was set in Dublin, Ireland refused to accept his body. He was buried in Zürich, eventually joined there by his wife and son.

Joyce's novels are stream-of-consciousness puzzles told in multiple and invented languages. His work is so strange, so complicated, that many readers find it too difficult to understand. Others regard his work as extraordinarily inspirational. His influence on modernist fiction continues to be significant.

"Bloomsday" is celebrated annually in Dublin and several other cities on June 16th. This is the date of Joyce's first walk with Nora, and the day Molly Bloom's story takes place in his famed novel *Ulysses.*

When **Norman Mailer** was a bottle a day bourbon drinker, he was reportedly a rude, snide, argumentative brute. When he stabbed his second wife with a penknife, he was in a state of drunken and drugged out psychosis. He smoked weed daily and popped drugs for energy and sleep. Yet he published more than thirty books, many essays and articles.

Born in New Jersey and raised in Brooklyn, Mailer was a small man, a tough New Yorker with a chip on his shoulder. He went to Harvard early, was drafted by the army and saw action in World War II. He pushed himself every day to write and publish and spread his views.

After his first book became a bestseller when he was 25, he hung onto the spotlight for the rest of his long life.

By the time he married his sixth and final wife, Mailer was 52 and claimed he wanted to stop juggling women, lying, cheating, and wasting time. He wanted to get more serious about his work and commit to monogamy, he said—something he had never done before.

But that didn't happen.

When he was saddled with multiple alimonies and had nine children to support, he found he could not earn enough from his writing. So he went on the lecture circuit, speaking at colleges and other venues. He warned about plastic and television, citing them as toxic to human life. In this and other ways, he was ahead of his time.

Mailer's views were controversial, his actions often under public scrutiny: he nearly killed one wife and bragged about beating some of the others; a convicted murderer he helped to get paroled killed again soon after release; Mailer instigated bar brawls and punched celebrities in public; he was drunk and disorderly at parties and events. He ran for mayor of New York on ridiculous platforms. He made movies that were panned, and wrote books that were scorned.

Still, he kept on writing (and drinking and having affairs) until his death at 84. At the burial, a young woman performing a striptease had to be removed from the cemetery. His widow called it "a very Norman Mailer funeral."

References

James Baldwin, *Notes of a Native Son,* Beacon Press, 1955.
Harold Bloom, Editor, *James Baldwin: Modern Critical Views,* Chelsea House, 1985.
James Campbell, *Talking at the Gates: A Life of James Baldwin,* University of California Press, 2021.
Blake Bailey, *Cheever: A Life,* Knopf, 2009.
Susan Cheever, *Home Before Dark: A Biographical Memoir of John Cheever by his Daughter*, Washington Square Books, 1984.
F. Scott Fitzgerald, *The Crack-Up*, New Directions, 2009.
Ruth Prigozy, *F. Scott Fitzgerald,* Overlook Press, 2001.
Nicholas Shakespeare, *Ian Fleming: The Complete Man,* Harper, 2024.
Nathan Ward, *The Lost Detective: Becoming Dashiell Hammett*, Bloomsbury USA, 2015.
Jo Hammett, *Hammett: A Daughter Remembers,* Carroll & Graff, 2001.
Mary V. Dearborn, *Ernest Hemingway: A Biography,* Vintage, 2018.
Gordon Bowker, *James Joyce: A New Biography,* Farrar, Straus and Giroux, 2012.
Edna O'Brien, *James Joyce: A Life*, Penguin, 2011.
Norris Church Mailer*, A Ticket to the Circus,* Random House, 2010.
Richard Bradford, *Tough Guy: The Life of Norman Mailer*, Bloomsbury, 2023.

Recommended Reading

James Baldwin, *Giovanni's Room*
James Baldwin, *Going to Meet the Man: Stories*
John Cheever, *The Stories of John Cheever*
John Cheever, *Bullet Park*
F. Scott Fitzgerald, *The Great Gatsby*
F. Scott Fitzgerald, *Babylon Revisited and Other Stories*
Ian Fleming, *Casino Royale*
Ian Fleming, *From Russia, With Love*
Dashiell Hammett, *Crime Stories and Other Writings*
Dashiell Hammett, *The Hunter and Other Stories*
Ernest Hemingway, *The Old Man and the Sea*
Ernest Hemingway, *A Moveable Feast*
James Joyce, *Dubliners*
Norman Mailer, *The Executioner's Song*
Norman Mailer, *The Armies of the Night*

Acknowledgments

Poems appeared in literary journals, sometimes in slightly altered form and under another (pen) name:

ANTAE:
James Baldwin: "The Poor Are Always Crossing the Sahara," "Trouble Means You're Alone"

Misfit Magazine:
"The Cheevers in Manhattan," "The Curious Case of Francis Scott Key Fitzgerald," "Dash," "The Wives of Norman Mailer"

WINK:
"Joyce's Dublin," "Joyce and Nora," "Joyce's Ulysses," Hemingway: "A Moveable Feast," "Key West," "The Old Man"

www.ingramcontent.com/pod-product-compliance
Ingram Content Group UK Ltd.
Pitfield, Milton Keynes, MK11 3LW, UK
UKHW041316190726
13845UKWH00025B/298

9 789363 544901